All Scripture references are from the KJV of the Bible, unless otherwise indicated.

Freshwater Press, USA

freshwaterpress9@gmail.com

Copyright 2002, 2022 by Dr. Marlene Miles

ISBN# 978-1-960150-04-2

Copyright 2022 by Dr. Marlene Miles

All rights reserved. No part of this book may be reproduced, distributed or transmitted by any means or in any means including photocopying, recording or other electronic or mechanical methods without prior written permission of the publisher except in the case of brief publications or critical reviews.

Table of Contents

- Congratulations, It's a Son 4
- Your Birthright...12
- The Fullness of the Earth 17
- The Seed 20
- The Seedling 23
- The Soil 27
- Unity 34
- Growing Seasons 40
- Streaked, Spotted or Speckled 44
- If Something Offends You 69
- Name Your Seed..73
- Motive 86
- Arise & Thresh...93
- Just the Two of Us 97
- Balancing It All...103
- Delivery Charges Apply 107
- Christian books by this author:.....................................115

Name Your Seed

Receiving 30, 60, and 100-fold returns

The Fold, Book 2

Freshwater Press

USA

Congratulations, It's a Son

(Portions of this chapter are excerpted and condensed from ***The Fold, Receiving 30, 60, and 100-Fold Returns***, Book 1 by this author.)

You have sown in the offering with *expectancy*. God has *received* your offering seed. Congratulations, you're a parent.

In the natural plan of marriage, a man who loves his wife will have occasion to sow a seed. The sowing is an act of worship, love, and adoration. The exact *sowing* event may or may not be forgotten, but the **seed** transcends time. That seed which is sown is presented to God with a sense of expectancy; it is *received* and prepared for **Multiplication**. God grows the seed, then presents it back to the couple. When fullness is reached, there's a harvest for that couple. That which was a seed has become a boy or a girl. God is in this because of the married couple's covenant, which GOD is also in.

Spiritually, when seed is sown in the Offering, it is a worship. God receives that Offering seed and it keeps on living, growing, it multiplies and produces offspring *after its kind*. In the natural, parents have responsibility to mature, grow their seed, offspring, or *son*. Spiritually, it's the same, but it's the only kind of "child" that will always bring you *more* than they cost, as long as you do your job and *parent* it.

But where do you get the Wisdom to parent your spiritual seeds? God shows you; He teaches you. He shows you by modeling it **for you**, to you and *in* **you**. Are there reminders that you are a parent? In the natural--, you're looking right at the baby or hearing it cry or coo, it's very easy, but *spiritually*, when there is not yet a manifestation of your parenthood, you need a presence of mind, a consciousness, a recall, or a remembrance, and faith that **you have become a parent**.

Seed that becomes a worship, will live.

The Holy Spirit is especially helpful in this. *That* you remember that you are a *parent* of spiritual seed is one of the biggest **substances** of your Faith. With Faith, your spiritual financial seed will be real, and remain real to you as it lives, grows, and multiplies spiritually even before it reaches fullness of for harvest in the natural.

Financial Offering seeds are very powerful. Those seeds are given authority and purpose after the tithe has been paid. They're given **power** when sown in faith, with *expectancy*. There should be expectancy in every seed you sow. After sowing, as you parent your seed, (your son) in the natural, once you find out you're *with child* there will be all sorts of things you will do or not do to prepare for being an example to your "child" that you're expecting or just gave birth to.

Congratulations, it's a *Son*.

In the spiritual, the secret to you shepherding your seed is your being shepherded by your pastor and ultimately the Good Shepherd. That's the key to guiding, gardening, and growing your seeds to full harvest. Shepherding is as parenting.

What joy when you're bouncing 30, 60, or 100-fold *son* is born-- preferably 100-fold because we all want wholeness, perfection, and fullness in our children and in everything that comes from us, and to us.

Many times, natural children are pretty much just like their parents were when they were conceived and raised. they are, very often a reflection of you. Your spiritual, monetary Offering *seed* will be just like **you** in the season of its sowing and growing. When it harvests, reaching maturity and fullness, it will look just like you do, spiritually speaking. That is, if you reach maturity and fullness in the area that God is dealing with you in right now. If you give up, faint-- then you won't, and your seed won't. If you don't press through and follow through, you won't reach the level of personal soul prosperity and your sowing will not attain to seed prosperity, which is what you need in order to harvest.

A poor harvest is deficient in whatever way you're deficient.

By allowing God to minister to you, you minister to your seed. By allowing God to minister to you, you minister to your *children*. As a parent, you instruct, teach and minister to your children. As you are also a child of God who continually needs to be parented, instructed, taught, and ministered to in order to reach both the next level and the Glory of God, so is your seed. As a parent, your example is how you model for your child. What you allow God *to do for you, to you, in you, and through you* will be reflected back *to you* in your seed(s), (natural and spiritual).

Always parent every seed. Husbandry is stewardship and we are called to be wise stewards over the works of God's hands. Do not orphan your seeds if you want to realize 30, 60 and 100-fold return in your sowing.

Ever see a farmer standing in the middle of a field with nothing in it. Ever see a farmer go back to a field with nothing in it, ***daily***? Then you've never seen a farmer doing what he <u>really</u> does. His going out to the "empty" fields, is the ***substance*** of what he hopes for, and that is Faith.

I plant gardens around my home. They are diagrammed. I know what plant, flower, bulb, and bush is where. I know what is expected next season and next year and what is not. I know what I have to replant in what season; I know what is annual, and what is perennial. I'm a gardener. If I were a farmer, I'd know what field my corn was in. And in what field my wheat is planted, and so on. I'd know approximately what day any seed was scheduled to come up, bloom, bear fruit and harvest. I'd check on it daily. After sowing, I'd go back to the field even before the seed came up, knowing and having full expectancy that the seed *would* come up. Most definitely, I'd have a good idea of *when*. This is why farmers stay home pretty much in the growing seasons. Expectancy. Don't you hang around to check on your crops, your bank accounts, investments, or have access to doing so even when you travel? A farmer can't check on those fields on vacation. That's why he's home most, or all of the year.

Ever see a pregnant woman who doesn't look pregnant take prenatal vitamins. That's the ***substance*** of what she hopes for. That's Faith. Even in the first trimester, before she begins to show, she checks her figure daily, as does the farmer in the planted field. At first it doesn't look like anything is in there, but they both know that there is.

Maybe you need to diagram your spiritual sowing. Since some of your planted spiritual seed hasn't come up or some may be delayed in coming up, you may need a journal of your sowing. I'd refer to this as a sowing journal. Like gardens, farmers, and pregnant ladies, you've got to know what supposed to come up, *when*. https://a.co/d/1jNLlB1

You should sow where you **live**. If you sow elsewhere, *with permission*, you've got to come back to see about your seed. Many people--, too many people don't come back to check on what they sowed. Not daily, not ever. They just sow it and wait for a miracle. Many fields are not empty, but no one came back to check for the growth or harvest; they left off working that field. If you're going to get your harvest by a miracle, you wouldn't need to sow, you could just sit around and wait for the miracle. Sowing is not a mystery, but realization of the harvest can be miraculous.

Your Birthright

If you want to sow in and harvest from the Offering, you need to be legitimately in the *Fold*. Instead of worrying about what Country Club you can get into, you'd do better to concern yourself about whether you're a member of the *Fold*. What Fold? The 30-Fold, the 60-Fold, or the 100-Fold of returns in the Offering.

What Fold can you get into? and can your kids get in? At what level?

Isaac received 100-fold return even in the time of famine, (Genesis 24). Jacob, Isaac's son, had his cattle to increase --, *how many fold* from Laban? The wealth of the wicked is laid up for the just, (Proverbs 13:22b). How was Laban unjust or wicked? Laban dealt falsely with

Jacob and was unprofitable, or wicked. A false balance is an abomination to the Lord, (Proverbs 11:1). When God says something is an abomination, that means that He really hates it.

How was Jacob *just*? The name, Jacob means, *deceiver*. But Jacob was prophetically *justified* by his granddaddy, Abraham, who was a tither. Subsequently Jacob's name was **changed** to Israel, which means, *prince*. You know a prince is the heir to a king. Again, see how blessed it is to be a child of the King, to be an heir. Jacob was justified by God, just as you are justified by your Father, God, and by the Righteousness of Christ. As a child (heir) of the King, you have **birthright** to the prosperity in the Earth, and <u>the Earth must give up its yield to you.</u>

You also have **birthright** access into the *Fold* if you are a tither. If you don't think so, if you think you were born wrong, then get reborn.

Jacob had a **birthright**, and he knew it It wasn't even that he was the oldest, Esau was, and the elder usually gets the whole inheritance. The birthright is because of who his daddy was. Esau also had the daddy and was born in the correct order, but he didn't *realize* the value of it. He did not think his lineage was valuable.

And Esau said, behold, I'm at the point to die; and what profit shall this birthright do to me?
Genesis 25:32

Who is your daddy, in the natural? Is he a tither? Are you born-again? Then you've got a birthright. Even if your natural daddy was not/is not a tither, if you've been reborn, then God is your new Daddy and you've got the birthright. Jesus had the birthright from the start. Think about those baby shower gifts that He got.

In the natural, ask your family and friends to bring gifts that will help your baby's *ministry*, and they will, of course, look at you, bewildered. But it's what the Wise Men did. They bought not only ministry gifts, they brought worthy gifts for a worthy ministry.

Abraham insured his children to the 4th generation into the *Fold* without ever paying life insurance premium: By tithing.

     Jesus didn't receive the Holy Spirit until He was 30. Some of you were Spirit-filled as teenagers. So, what are you waiting for? Gifts such as the Wise Men brought? Thirty years later, Jesus' ministry began proving that those Wise Men were indeed prophets. Are you still waiting for your baby shower gifts so you can have funds for your ministry? Get real. *(You are real, aren't you?)* Your ministry is waiting on finances, isn't it? How about 30, 60, 100-fold return in the sowing? Would that help you? Now that can happen. That is a ***birthright*** gift that keeps on giving. And since you already have the Holy Spirit, it's time to get out there and do some ministry.

When you're born right,

because of your birthright, you will profit.

Do you know any prophets? Invite them to your baby shower. They give the best gifts. You know they have the prophets' reward with them if you *receive* them.

Which brings us to another point: Obey the prophets and you will prosper. A church, that is moving in all the gifts of the five-fold ministry should be more profitable than one that is not. **Prosperity is tied to the prophets.** The widow woman at Zarephath can vouch for this, as can the widow with the two sons; bottom line is, whomever obeyed the prophets, prospered.

The Fullness of the Earth

Moreover, the profit of the earth is for all; the king himself is served by the field. Ecclesiastes 5:9

The Earth is full and is commanded to yield Her fruit to you, in the land that God gives you. Therefore, you should not lack. Are you in the right land? Are you where the LORD says you're supposed to be? Did God give you that land? Is the Earth of that land YIELDING Her fruit to you?

Blessed are the peacemakers, for they shall be called the children of God. Matthew 5:9

Peacemaker. You are a child of God; you have a **birthright** in the 100-Fold.

Who are you to God?

Isaac received 100-fold return even in the time of famine. Why? Because he had a birthright to it. He had a right for the land to yield to him. Levi tithed in Abraham. Abraham's tithing was accounted as faith and righteousness unto him and he tithed to his 3rd and 4th generations. Abraham ensured his children to the 4th generations into the *Fold* without ever paying a life insurance premium. How did he do that? By tithing. Are you the child of a tither? Are you the *seed* of a tither? Talk about inheritance to the *children's* children. Your ancestor was a good man/woman!

What is your *title* in the Kingdom? Are you walking in it? How are you ***living*** when you think you're out of God's presence? Where do you *live* Monday through Saturday? Where do you *live* on Sunday? Where do you *live* 24/7? One born into royalty in the Kingdom ***lives*** as one who is in the Kingdom. One who **<u>knows</u>** what his **birthright** is *lives* accordingly.

Children of God do not want, they do not lack, they do not suffer insufficiency; His children are provided for. God is Father. Fathers provide. Sheep in the *Fold* of the Lord do not suffer without; they are provided green pastures and still waters. Those who are the *called,* the children of God by birthright and adoption shall also prosper. **Birthright** gives you the right to the 100-fold return in your sowing.

The blessing of the Lord maketh rich, and he addeth no sorrow with it. (Proverbs 10:22)

The Seed

Whew! Look at all it took for you to sow, and that was just the first part. Now the dangers to your seed rear their ugly heads. Some of that seed will get choked, some will fall to the wayside, some will begin to prosper and then dry up in the sun. Which seed falls on the wayside? Which seed is choked? Which seed? Why some 30? Why some 60? Why some 100-fold return? God has already begun to answer those questions, and we are learning that it is related to the *profitability* and fruitfulness of the Sower. And those things are related to the Sower's spirit, soul, and lifestyle.

The seed of the tither will prosper. The seed of the profitable and righteous will prosper. God will deliver the seed of the Righteous. That means He will prosper to fullness and give it into your hands.

*Where is this **received** seed supposed to grow?* Some seed falls to the wayside. Hard-hearted people can't receive seed--, the seed of the Word. The seed of the hard-hearted falls on stony ground. The hard-hearted have hard soil because the heart is the soil.

I thought God *received* the seed, you may ask? Yes, He does.

In the natural after all of your success in what you are going through will be reflected in the harvest of that spiritual seed you sowed at church on Sunday that correlates to *why* you sowed it.

So back to the hard hearts. They must yield to God for softening before reaping in the 30, 60, or 100-fold levels. Hate, bitterness, unforgiveness, and other works of the flesh, (Galatians 5:19-21) stop seeds cold in their tracks. If you're harboring hate, animosity, and any other work of the flesh that hardens and corrupts the heart, and you can expect no return from your sowing; you can just rename your attempts at sowing to only *giving*.

Fallow ground has been plowed or tilled, but it still has no seed. A fallow soul has heard the Word but has not received any seed. Perhaps the seed was not received because of hardness, maybe it was because of slack faith or some other reason, but there is no seed in it.

Your land or field corresponds to your soul or heart. Let's say you do receive some seed; it may start to grow then somewhere in that growing season there is a long, hot summer, a season of adversity, and the tests were not passed. When you were going through, did you continue to praise and worship the Lord? If your worship dried up, your seed did too. No matter what you're going through, the prospering soul knows to keep praising the Lord, (Psalm 43:5). The prosperity of your seed will mirror the prosperity, or the lack thereof, of your soul. Because of prospering souls, the seed of some grow to 30, and 60-fold, some to fullness, and maturity at 100-fold.

The Seedling

Seedlings, (baby plants) need to be staked and steadied so that they are not tossed about with every wind of doctrine, just the same way you need to be anchored and assured in the Word, so you are undaunted during the growing season of your harvest and *your* growing season. **You** need to be steady in order to properly minister to your seed.

Horizontally, you need to have the correct sheep-to- sheep connection with a 30, 60, or 100-fold *return* to come to you. In farming terms, one plant can't be too close to the other. And plants can't be too far away from each other either. Your correct sheep-to-sheep relationship means you can't be too far away from the other sheep, or crowding them out for food, water, and nutrients. When you respect the other sheep of the Fold, (the other members of your congregation), disrespect won't be an impediment in receiving 30, 60, and 100-fold return in your sowing.

When you prosper your soul, you prosper in your *Fold*.

The Plant (Vine)

Vines bear fruit. Fruit is the harvest. When you're bearing good fruit in your spirit it is evident as the Fruits of the Spirit. When you are increasing in your soul the evidence of that increase is called soul prosperity. And that means three things:

1. You planted (sowed seeds).
2. Your spirit man is growing and maturing.
3. You prospered or are prospering in your soul.

Your spiritual and soul's vine is the heavenly mirror to your vine in the natural. As you prosper in your soul, you will have better health and more wealth, (3 John 2). When you prosper in your soul, you prosper in your *fold*. As you prosper in your spirit you become more like Christ and your spiritual connection to God is more assured. When your spiritual hookup is assured, your seeds are *received* and then set for the maturation process.

Your vine should be bearing fruit. In the natural your vines would bear apples, grapes and the like, if you were a farmer. In the natural as you do your work, your fruits are the results of whatever you do as your professional career. When you're doing the work of an evangelist, you as the branch, as you are connected to Christ who is the Vine, should be bearing fruit of the field that is white to harvest. That means your fruit, your harvest is *people* (souls). You bear them up as baby Christians until they can stand on their own. Natural and spiritual fruit should be born of you because of your being in the Earth and your connection to Christ.

Remember, life is in the connecting. You have authority in the Earth and because of Christ, you have authority in the heavenlies as well. You should be bearing fruits of evangelism, professional fruit, whatever you do that gets you that gold watch for working there 50 years, *and* financial fruit.

The little foxes spoil the vine, (Song of Solomon 2:15). In the spiritual, little foxes are such as fiery darts of the enemy, agitations and distractions that keep you from ministering to your seed properly, or at all. Little foxes cause real setbacks and if not addressed they can compound, completely ruining the vine and the harvest.

We admire those who prosper. If we're shallow, we admire them because they are prospering. If we're deeper we admire them because of their maturity level in God, which is reflected by their outward prosperity.

The Soil

In the natural, there are unprofitable things regarding seed, sowing, and having seed in the ground that you should know about. Avoid things such as no soil, wrong soil, bad soil, and rocky terrain. Covering up the plant with too much soil, is evidenced by weighed down and choked out seeds that don't come up, much less produce the desired, and sometimes needed harvest. Other problems could be, no fertilizer, no mulch, or the wrong season; in such cases, you can expect other delays and disappointments. There's so much to know. To be a successful farmer, you learn about soil, climate, seed, cultivating, watering, fertilizing, mulching, pruning, staking, harvesting, et cetera. As a sower of seed in the Offering, what have you learned about spiritual financial sowing? About 20 to 50% of Christians have learned to listen to the man or woman of God when they say it's time to sow. About 20% hear and obey what *amount* of seed to sow. Somewhere between 1% and 5% hear and obey God about *when, how,* and *how much* to sow.

And I will break the pride of your power, and I will make your heaven as iron, and your earth is brass. And your strength shall be spent in vain, and your land shall not yield her increase, neither shall the trees of the land yield. They're fruits, (Leviticus 26:19-20).

Spiritually, there are many concerns as well. For example, covering a seed with too much soil means there's too much flesh in your life. That means any work of the flesh--, pride, jealousy, anger. It could mean *fear* is present. The soil of the land may be barren and dry because of a shut-up heaven. If heaven is not flowing down revelation, Wisdom, and direction, the soil will not be ministered to. You are the soil.

It could be that the *soil* is rejecting the ministry that God is sending. You have free will to yield to or reject the Lord, and God can reject you in your rebellion or disobedience, which are both *unprofitable*. God says of the land, (soil) that is full of pride of its power that land will not yield increase and trees will not yield their fruit.

Farmers know about land, soil, climate, (including weather abnormalities), seed, seasons, tending, watering, cultivating, fertilizing, mulching, pruning, staking, pollination, cross-pollination, harvesting, insects, natural enemies of the plants, crop rotation. If you think farmers aren't smart, that shows how smart you are. *Spiritual* farmers also have to be spiritually smart.

In the case of land that is not yielding, maybe the land needs help. Heal the land. God says He will heal the land if His people who are the called by His name, would humble themselves and pray, seek His face and turn from their wicked ways, (2 Chronicles 7:14). Bad spiritual soil requires healing, for this healing, repentance is needed. Repentance is very profitable.

Issues such as the right to use of land (ownership) must come up. God gave land to people throughout the Bible. Most of what any fighting is about, even today, is land and territory. Do you remember the song, *Exodus* from the 1960s? Some of the lyrics are, *"This land is mine. God gave this land to me."* When God gives people a land, the land is expected, anointed, and <u>authorized</u> to yield for them--, both the natural and spiritual land.

Spiritually, does God have the right to use *your* land? To improve it? To grow it? To harvest on it? Does God have access to you? Full access, or are you sharecropping? Got fields of godly seed commingled with seeds of sin? What happens on **your** land to seeds that God plants *in you* corresponds to what happens to your financial seeds that you sow, and what will manifest in the natural.

What happens on a land, even a land that God gives, determines how it receives and bears seed that is introduced into it. If the land is cursed by God, cursed by sin, or cursed by blood being shed on it--, murder, then it will not bear the same amount of fruit and harvest as land that is *given* by the Lord, cleansed, and ordained by God for the people who are on it. And it should be properly kept (dressed). God gives lands to people, He gives them authority to use it, and He establishes and commands the land to bless them. God commands the Earth to yield of its fruit to those with whom He is well-pleased.

As you are being planted in a church, even though **you** are considered land or soil to God, you should ask and learn the answers to questions such as: *What grows well in this soil (the soil of this church)? What does this soil have anointing or Grace to grow?*

If you're not getting the harvest you expect, perhaps crop rotation is needed. Do you keep sowing the same seed season after season? —the God, *I-need-more-money* seed and God, *I-want-more-money* seed. Don't you think that God is tired of that? How many Mo' Money Fields do you think there are? How many do you think are available to you, and at what intervals? Or do you believe that Fields are like wild cards, and you can name them whatever you want, whenever you want? No, they're not, and no, you cannot. So, in a worn out or nonexistent field, you'll reap nothing. Sow for what? Sow for what the Field is anointed to yield, and at the appropriate time.

Wisdom tells you what, when, and where to plant. Obedience gets it planted. Here's a hint: Properly naming your seed will help it come to fullness. **Name your seed the same name as the Field in which it is sown.**

Having the right soil, good soil, the right to use the land, but using the wrong seed, or planting in the wrong season, or where there is no spiritual anointing for what you want, or need will not bring harvest. For example, Singles, is this the right season to sow for a mate, or should you be sowing for your college degree? You need an anointing or a prophetic word--, maybe through your pastor, as well as Wisdom to sort this out. Then you need obedience to mix with your Faith.

When the Man of God says it's time in the Spirit to sow for new business ideas, God has just authorized the use of the *New Business* Fields. Right now! Sow! Even if you don't think or want or need a new business idea today, plant the crop, so it'll be there when you need it or when your child needs it. God who is All-Knowing would not authorize the use of a Field unless you need it and we're about to need it or would need it sometime in the future.

Not sowing in available spiritual fields is unprofitable. Sowing in unauthorized fields is unprofitable.

Unity

The Bible keeps giving us *keys*. Unity is a big key. Unity helps heal the land and it keeps it healed. What the people do on the land is critical. Fellowship and relationship are important. The family, the father and the son must get along or *God will smite the earth with a curse (Mal 4)*. The pastor is the father; the member is the son. If you think you can be in a church where you don't like the pastor, the father and receive 30, 60, and 100-fold you must be joking. If you think you can be in a church where the father doesn't care for you, ditto.

(Further, any relationship other than father-son in the pastor-member dynamic is perverted. Perversion is not of God.)

What is released over the land goes up to make up the cloud cover over the atmosphere of any land. Flying frequently, I look out the window at 35,000 feet to see clouds. Have you ever wondered what's in clouds? When a cloud gets heavy enough, it'll rain. What will it rain? Whatever was sent up, into that cloud. If it's disharmony and discord, that's what will rain down. Disharmony and discord is poison to the seed in the ground beneath it. Unless there's repentance, that rained-down poison will kill plants and there will be no harvest.

Repentance is very profitable.

Repentance is very good for the land, repeating (2 Chronicles 7:14), *If my people who are the **called** of my name would humble themselves and pray, turn from their wicked ways, then will I heal their land.*

God wants to heal our lands. He wants to heal the places that He's given us, our cities, and towns, and He also wants to heal us individually. God receives the humble and those of a contrite heart. God must heal our land in order for us to prosper. If a land is sick, the people will soon follow. A sick, land won't yield. And that's best, because if it did, that would be sick fruit. If people are sick, the land will soon follow.

When there's strife between brothers in a congregation the Word says, *If your brother has ought against you, leave your gift and go make peace with your brother and then come back to make your offering,* (Matthew 5:23). God's not accepting your offering as long as you're fighting with one another. There can be no flesh in the Offering seed; get all works of the flesh out of you before sowing. If God's not accepting or *receiving* it, it ain't growing. If it ain't growing, there's nothing to harvest. Do your part to heal the land individually and corporately.

Good soil is spiritually uncursed, blessed soil given by God to people who live in unity and harmony as much as possible. The sins of the father are repented of and atonement has been made, the hearts of the fathers and the sons are reconciled. So, there's no curse, there's prosperity, (Mal 4:5-6).

What does that mean in a church? Are you sitting in a renegade on sanctioned, unblessed, unauthorized church? Or was this church ordained of God? Was it sanctioned by the spiritual father, the founder, or the previous administration of this church? Was this pastor *sent*? Was he blessed; is he blessed? Here's a clue: Was he *sent* and is this expansion is blessed by the spiritual father, that is, the father in the Gospel and are they still properly connected? Or, at least, were they connected for some time after this church began?

If the vine has no connection root wise, it cannot bear. If it has no exposure to the sunlight it cannot bear. Is this church authorized by God or is it a fly-by-night set up? Is this church ordained and sanctioned by God? Look at the harvests.

What does this have to do with you? Everything. It affects everything about you and your home, from relationships to prosperity. Are you in a blessed church? If the spiritual father and son don't get along, then maybe there was a church split. Or is there another spiritual father? Authority has come up again as well as accountability.

And what is your relationship in all of this? As a spiritual son, Malachi speaks of the need for the father's and the son's, hearts to be mended toward one another, for the land to be uncursed that is, healed. Much prayer, repentance, Wisdom, and guidance from God is needed.

If you were adopting a child, the adoption agency and Courts would check out you and your spouse's relationship, as well as your relationships to your respective parents and families. The agency might evaluate the homes you all came from, as well as how you parent any other children that you may already have in in the home. If you're seeking a *spiritual* father and mother, don't you check out those same things when choosing a church? Or do you just join if you like the singing or the preaching? We are in a new day, and your spiritual home cannot be chosen for you by your grandmother or because you like the location. Neither can it be based solely on surface things. That is, if you are truly a disciple of Christ planning to be fitly joined to the Body of Christ, allow God to direct you and plant you.

Are you in a church with a healed land? Yes. Praise God.

No? Then no wonder your seeds seem to be going down the drain.

If the answer is, No, don't run out of the door just yet. If you're there, and you're also reading this book, then perhaps God is calling you to pray. Pray what? Pray for the healing of the land of your church. Pray for the reconciliation and relationship of your spiritual father with his spiritual father and natural father also, for that matter. You all will be immeasurably blessed. You can't just run out for green or fatter pastures.

There are no perfect churches in the world--, not yet.

Growing Seasons

How are you sowing? You don't sow seed by throwing it off a Cliff. It is sown out of your hands and agreement with God or the power of your hands. The seed must be sown and that power will cause *Increase* to come to you. Your hands have God-given power. He does not need you to try to create what He's already created, but to make it better. *Sowing* the seed makes it better and more profitable than if it's shut up in the barn.

We are promised to be able to do greater things, (John 14:12). Jesus, I remind you, got a 100-fold return on everything, even when He sowed for fish on dry land!

A sown seed of $100, for example, will increase to 3,000., 6,000., even $100,000. Looking at those numbers, I ask you again. Are you getting the right return on your sowing? Also, 100-fold return doesn't mean exactly 100 times. It means, *to completeness, to completion, fullness, more than enough*--, an El-Shaddai-type blessing. It could mean more than 100 times.

As a farmer, I know the season in which to plant any crop, else I wouldn't plant. I wouldn't waste the investment in seed, and time without knowing what to do next. How long will it take for this *son* to reach wholeness? Fullness? Nine month? Nine days? Nine years? Don't know? It depends on:

The season you sowed it in.

What you sowed it for.

You, the maturity of your spirit and the prosperity of your soul.

Your faith in any number of things that we've discussed or will discuss in this book or entire **The Fold**, 4-book series.

My point is, since we're sowing for spiritual things, you really don't know *when* your seed will reach fullness except by a Word from the Lord, or by the receiving the actual return. So, the best response is to **always be expecting** the perpetually pregnant but be constantly harvesting as well.

(Adds a new meaning to the alleged myth that the Hebrew women gave birth in the fields.) Always be expecting and also harvesting at the same time.)

The returns of your Offerings should never go down. They should always be going up if you're doing it right, if you're living right. But it's not a perfect world yet. People in the Body of Christ should be increasing in return in their giving. Their respective tithes and offerings should be increasing as well. Churches should be waxing stronger and bolder financially because returns in the Offerings should be increasing for the Body of Christ. Unfortunately, that doesn't seem to be what's happening.

(Get more copies of this book and ***Power Money: 9X the Tithe*** and give them to people you know and love. Your spiritual brothers and sisters help them to increase in their returns.)

Streaked, Spotted or Speckled

Here's that word, *unprofitable* again. Now that you've sown your seed and become a parent, here's a good rule to live and profit by: Anything that is unprofitable to your natural life, godliness, or soul, is not profitable to your seed. Anything that profits your life, godliness, or soul profits your harvest. No matter what these profitable or unprofitable things do to your body, consider the soul and spirit foremost when making choices. Your flesh, if you're giving it an inch, it will try to take over your life. If any part of your being could be called your enemy, it would be your flesh. Don't hate it, love it, but love it, right.

Make friends with your soul. Get to know it and cause it to prosper. Your soul is sometimes referred to as your heart. Out of your heart (soul) come the issues of life. Nourish your soul and feed your spirit with the Word of God. Keep the Word of God.

For circumcision verily profiteth, if thou keep the law; but if thou be a breaker of the law, thy circumcision is made uncircumcision. Romans 2:25

Circumcision of the mind profits very much. Once your mind is opened, and information is given to you, you become accountable for it. If you know better, but do what you want anyway, your harvest will be diminished or destroyed. With everything that is in you and with the help of the Holy Spirit, keep the Word of God.

Sexual Sin

Two big seed killers are sexual sin and sins of money, especially in dealing with other people and other people's money.

And this I speak for your own profit, not that I may cast a snare upon you, but for that which is comely, and that you may attend upon the Lord without distraction, but if any man thinks that he behaveth himself uncomely toward his virgin, if she passed the flower of her age and need so require, let him do what he will, he sinneth not, let them marry. 1 Corinthians 7:35-36

Sexual sin (illegal sex) is sin against **Multiplication**. If you sin sexually while you are the parent of a financial spiritual seed, your 30, 60, or 100-fold return may automatically and dramatically have problems. After sexual sin, God throws the circuit breaker to turn off **Multiplication**.

O-F-F!

Adam and Eve were in a 100-fold Garden when they sinned against Covenant. So don't tell me anything about apples. Anyway, God threw the circuit breaker and got them **out** of the 100-fold Garden, out of

Multiplication. He even posted a warrior angel at the entrance so they wouldn't sneak back in.

Here's the enemy's trick, no pun intended. Fornicators and adulterers put themselves in the act of actively participating, actively practicing, **not wanting to multiply.** To sex outlaws, *multiplying* would mean **getting caught**. They may be actively speaking verbal agreements such as, *No babies*, or *No children*. They might as well say, **No Multiplication**, and *No harvests*. As they make their sin covenants and soul ties, they are saying verbally and nonverbally to God, *No fruit* as they participate in their fruitless encounters.

Then it's Sunday again, as their declarations all week or weekend have been, *No fruit*, why are either of them taking out their wallet or checkbook? Oh, I know--, for gift giving because there's no sowing going on here. Maybe they'd like to see what it would be like to have their lukewarm seed spit out of God's mouth. How did it get lukewarm? They are hot for each other, hot for sin and cold for God. Add it up. That equals lukewarm.

No fruit is why Jesus cursed the fig tree. Further, choosing sin puts men under the Curse of the Law and under the Curse is barrenness, unproductivity, or unfruitfulness. Until repentance and cleansing, man remains under the Curse and unfruitful. So goes a hopeful return from his sowing. Yes, personal deliverance would help most people's *return* in their offerings.

Some of those sexual sins that need to be repented of are abominations to God as two who can never have fruit from their 'relationship' continue to engage in it. Perverse relationships can **never** bear fruit. The devil doesn't bear fruit; he must recruit. If the devil could bear any kind of fruit, he would have invited Adam and Eve into *his* garden, but he didn't have one.

You can sow till the cows come home, but if you fall into sin, especially sexual sin, you will mess up your harvest, big time. Jacob's harvest from Laban's cows and goats and lambs were streaked, spotted, and speckled, (Genesis 31:8). As cows and cattle are considered great harvests in the Bible, let's look at them as something desirable to have for the purpose of this book. Even if you're not a farmer or rancher, if you fall into sexual sin while awaiting your harvest, as said before you could sow until the cows come home, because your cows may not ever come home. Your harvest, exemplified by the cows, may not ever manifest. You may never realize your harvest, no spotted, no speckled, no streaked cows--, nothing. Invisible.

The Israelites in the Wilderness had money in great spoils, but they fell into:

Idolatry.

Sexual sin.

Disobedience.

Murmuring.

Complaining, and

Disrespected authority, (man's and God's).

So, they did not enter into the Promised Land. They did not enter into the Promise. This Promised Land was to be dripping with milk and honey, which sounds like a paradise, and a Fat Pasture. It sounds like a place where prosperity was probably at 100% or 100-fold, but they didn't *enter in*. Take the lesson here. Sexual sin is a real no-no when trying to harvest bountifully **from the Lord**.

I am not saying that ALL MULTIPLICATION is turned off when sexual sin happens. If God turns multiplication off, don't you think the devil will turn it on, to multiply toward his agenda? Even if roses aren't growing in your garden, won't there still be weeds?

Illicit sex invites and permits the devil into a counterfeit covenant/soul tie with your *right swipe or Mr. or Ms. Right Now*. When the devil is involved, he will do whatever is most devastating to the perpetrators and whatever is most advantageous to him. I am saying that sexual sin is a real no-no when trying to harvest GOOD THINGS and harvest bountifully from the LORD.

Also, add idolatry, disobedience, murmuring, complaining, and disrespecting authority and you may see some things that may help you understand why you may not be receiving 100-fold in every Offering that you have sown in, especially since you are a diligent tither. It may also give you some things to repent about right now, before your next opportunity to sow in the Offering.

What 'Cha Looking At?

Jacob's cows were streaked, speckled, and spotted. Laban chose which ones Jacob should have. Traditionally, those colors and patterns were the lesser in number. It's kind of like a slick child telling another you can have all the nickels and pennies because they are bigger, and I'll take the dimes because, they're smaller. *"Jacob,"* Laban probably said to him, *"You can take the spotted, speckled, and streaked ones, and I'll take the plain ones."* Being under Laban's authority, did Jacob have a choice? Jacob accepted, but he didn't fall for the trick. He used Wisdom and faith to become wealthy.

When Jacob's cattle were at the watering hole, they looked at what they should become, as Jacob had put spotted, speckled, and streaked sticks up for their viewing. These sticks eliminated self-esteem issues and identity crises, and the cattle and flocks multiplied after what they saw.

Like Jacob's cattle, what are you looking at? Whatever it is, it's what you will be. It's what your seed will be. If you're looking at a secret and undercover, fruitless relationship that you're trying to keep on the down low, your harvest will be on the downlow too. The percent of return will be down, and the harvest will be very low, if it even exists at all. Just as the cattle reproduced what they saw before them. Much like an artist's canvas becomes filled with the image of the model that he is studying. What you're looking at will produce itself in your life and will show up in your harvest, sooner or later.

For he that soweth to his flesh shall of the flesh reap corruption, but he that sell it to the spirit, shall of the Spirit reap life. Everlasting.
Galatians 6:8

What are you looking at today? Which Kingdom today? Prosperity or lack? Abundance or want? Whatever you keep your eyes focused on is what you will have, get, or become. Are you looking on the things of God, or is an idol consuming your attention and time?

Whatever your seed is named is what you should be looking on. Is there a sexual temptation catching your eye? That eye candy can't **multiply** seed and it can take away from what you already have. As a matter of fact, that temptation can *Un*-**multiply**, even destroy seeds, seedlings, and harvests completely. Temptations are distractions to keep you from realizing harvests up to 100-fold that the Lord intends for you.

God was trying to establish prosperity in Jacob so He could establish covenant with him. Why did it take Jacob all those years to leave Laban? Jacob was looking for a wife, wives, and women but Jacob had a certain destiny. God was looking to change Jacob's name. Jacob was looking to change Rachel's last name.

Jacob's name was going to be changed from *Deceiver* to **Israel**. Thank God for the name change. Destiny wasn't going to happen to a poor, broke man, especially coming from the loins of Abraham and Isaac. His father and grandfather had made too many sacrifices with their seed to fall apart now. And if God made him, *Prince* while he was broke, what would that mean for us? What about the legacy that he was to leave? What would he have been? The Prince of the Poverty?

No, thank you.

For more than 20 years Jacob was with Laban, after seven years, the number of perfection, he married Leah, instead of Rachel, the pretty one. Instead of Jacob then focusing his attention on his wife and all those male heirs Leah was giving him, and becoming prosperous so he could establish Covenant with God he was lusting after and working hard for Rachel.

Jacob didn't realize prosperity until he got his sexual, excuse me, *love* desires together with tending to Leah who birthed him six boys, Reuben, Simeon, Levi, Judah, Issachar, Zebulun, and a girl, Diana. And her maidservant Zilpha, mother of Gad and Asher. He had to make time for his favorite, Rachel. Rachel gave Jacob her maidservant Bilhah, who birthed Dan and Naphtali, two more sons. Finally, Rachel gave birth to Joseph and Benjamin. It wasn't until all this conjugating was completed that Jacob even got his mind on prosperity. Rachel was his focus, but his sex life was very active. All those children. You can't just blame the women, Jacob participated. All the while Jacob was dealing in his flesh, what he was thinking about, he reproduced. What was he looking at?

Flesh.

Two wives, two maidservants--, flesh. All this led to 12 boys and a girl. All flesh.

Further, Jacob's first 10 seeds, his natural children were not properly ministered to because he was so focused on Rachel. This played out later as the older boys resented their favorite seed, Joseph and sold him. After that, Benjamin was recognized as Jacob's favorite. When you don't properly minister to your seed in the natural, it messes it up. When you don't minister to financial seed, in the spiritual is as it though you orphan that seed, and it will not prosper to harvest.

Jacob was finally able to put his mind on his children when he took it off his obsession, the eye candy, Rachel.

Joseph, as a ministered-to seed was a great harvest to his father, Israel (Jacob). The others, while they were all still leaders of the tribes of Israel, didn't prosper like Joseph. Joseph's children even received in the inheritance.

And it's a good thing that polygamy was legal then, else Jacob and Rachel would have turned out more like David and Bathsheba, more sin, death, and other delays in fulfilling the Promise. David resorted to murder for the lust of his flesh. I've already gone into how Jacob's older boys were affected by his seven years of sexual distraction. Excuse me? Love distraction.

So, what's on your mind? What are you looking at? Lusting for? Do you want to wait *another* seven years to receive your true prosperity in God and establish covenant? Do you want your children to be messed up in the process of you *slowly* dealing with your flesh issues? Do you want your financial seeds that you've sown, that you're supposed to be parenting in the spiritual to be affected negatively? Do you want them to be lost to you completely? Then keep playing around.

Women *may* be better at it, more inclined to sowing and harvesting blessings, because at least in times past, they were not as susceptible to sexual temptation and sin as men. Of course, that was then, and this is now....

Sexual sin is another reason God tells us not to covet. To covet means to first look on something. It means to look on something that you're not supposed to look at, or something that you're not supposed to want or have. Then the decision to have that thing comes if it is not something you should have permanently it's not something you should want. If it's not attainable legally, there's no reason to look on it. If God says, *No*, then there's no reason to keep looking at it. Whatever God says don't look at but you study, meditate on or look on with lust and desire, you will eventually reach for it, or *become it* as it destroys you.

Enemy destructions are always pleasant to the eye, else they wouldn't be distractions.

I've spent a lot of time asking God why sexual sin is so offensive to Him. Foremost, it violates Covenant. It counters and negates **Multiplication.** And the subject of another book is that it is the easiest and most common way demons get into humans and into their lives. Sexual sin is an abomination to God. Illegal sex doesn't include God, but it includes demons, soul ties, evil covenants and impending disaster.

If we look at the abominations of God, we will see that 20% are related to sexual sin, 15% is related to idolatry and witchcraft, 10% is related to offerings. The other 55% are related to personality and character. Of that 55 percent, 40% are related to money, and especially in dealing with other people, as it relates to money. You draw the conclusions here. Here are the references.

Homosexual sin. Leviticus 20:13.

Graven images, or the gold or silver from which they are made. Deuteronomy 7:25.

Idolatry, serving other *gods*. Deuteronomy 13:14.

Bringing up damaged or blemished offering, low quality offering. Deuteronomy 7:1, Proverbs 15:8.

Divination, entrancing, witchcraft, Charmer, Wizard. Deuteronomy 18:10-12.

Crossdressing. Deuteronomy 22:5.

Prostitution money. Proverbs 23:18.

Remarrying the person, you divorced. Deuteronomy 24:4

False balance, lying in business. Deut 25:14-16. Prov 20:10, 20:23.

Froward-hearted people, Proverbs 3:32.

Pride. Proverbs 6:17, Proverbs 16:5.

Lying tongue. Proverbs 6:17.

Hands that shed innocent blood. Proverbs 6:17.

Heart that devises wicked imaginations. Proverbs 6:18, and 15;26.

False witness, perjury. Proverbs 6;19.

Quick to run to mischief. Proverbs 6:18.

Sowing discord among the brethren. Proverbs 6:19.

Obstinance, rebellion contrariness. Proverbs, 11:20.,

Condemning the innocent, letting the guilty go. Proverbs 17:5.

Wicked men and their sacrifices. Proverbs 21:27.

Fornication and adultery with any number of people, thy neighbor's wife, the daughter-in-law, ones sister's are equally foul. Proverbs 22;11.

Hiring a hitman. Ezekiel 22:12.

Extortion. Ezekiel 22:12.

Usry oppressing the poor. Ezekiel 18:12.

Looking at the list of what is an abomination to God, I was saddened by how wicked man is. But that's for God to judge. I was not particularly impressed that any sin is worse than another, since sin is sin. But I was losing sleep over something the Holy Spirit wanted to tell me, so I chose to listen. Sexual sin is abominable to God because as we look in Genesis, we see that our God is a covenant-making, and covenant-keeping God. He wants to establish covenant with us. The establishing of Covenant is very intimate. It is also life-giving when you accept it with God.

Or it can be like-taking if you establish covenant with the wrong entity or wrong folks. Illegal sex is the enemy's counterfeit of making covenant. It mocks God. It does not create covenant. It creates soul ties, illegal sex = illegal covenant = soul ties.

Whenever you have sex with anyone, you make covenant with them. What do you do when it's a one-night stand and then another opportunity presents? Break covenant? Evil, sin-covenants are usually not thought of again, until something really bad happens in a person's life. Those who *swipe right* just wipe their mouths and move on as if nothing has happened to them. If they are sinners, the unsaved, they are doing exactly what they are supposed to be doing.

But we, the saved, the called, God's people are not supposed to be doing any of that. Our God hates broken covenant, but how do you honor a covenant that's supposed to include only two people until the end of the Earth when you've made five, 10, 25 of them in your lifetime, through sex? And how many demons are in those 5, 10, 25 or more counterfeit covenants? I'm asking, how many soul ties, how many fragments of your soul are out there somewhere in the universe?

How many other agreements have you made and with how many other folks, that you haven't kept? And with how many other folks that you haven't kept, how many have you been forced to keep even though you broke the covenant. Been in court before a judge in the courts lately—from breaching contracts?

So, that latest contract you've made, is it really a covenant or is it just a soul tie? You must break soul ties. Warning: Both, or either party of a soul tie may not have the ability to break the tie, if one party insists on hanging on. That's why folks are moping and wandering around with broken hearts by the millions. That's what's wrong with a lot of people--, even in the Body, they are broken hearted. That's what the afternoon talk shows are all about--, broken hearts and soul ties, and no one knows what to do about it, really. God does, and Wisdom knows that God does.

Thankfully, God provided a special anointing to heal the brokenhearted, (Isaiah 61:1). People are so important to God, and He loves us so much that He provides this special anointing for hurting hearts. And because He knew how tough it would be to get over broken hearts that He provided a power for this needed healing.

How many brokenhearted people do you know who are properly ministering to their own natural seeds--, their children? Do you think they are ministering to their financial, seeds sown in the Offering, spiritually?

Broken hearts, soul ties and illegal covenants is a huge business for the devil. It's called *distraction* and the devil is the chief executive officer, owner, and operator. How many brokenhearted people do you know who are serving God with their **whole** hearts, their **whole** soul? None. Healing must come first. Soul ties and devil distractions are very negative because you need your whole soul to serve God and *parent* your seed, but instead because of illegal sex covenants and soul ties, your mind might be on what Johnny is doing, or where he is, or fantasizing about pornography. All the while the lust demon, a *spirit of lust* has caused you to abandon and orphan, your seed.

Sexual sin destroys **seed**. Sexual purity gives life to seed. Sexual purity is the result of an *excellence of spirit*. It is what produces a righteous seed, so that God will receive your Offerings. You have relations with your spouse for the purpose of creating life, usually--, but two non-spouses have illicit relations for *fun*. Onan was supposed to create an heir for his deceased brother, with Tamar, but chose to spill the seed. For this sexual disobedience Onan was killed. David and Bathsheba lost their first born because of sexual sin, deceit, and murder on David's part. Adam and Eve got kicked out of prosperity, out of paradise because they ate an apple? Get real. They entered into some kind of covenant with that devil, and we know it was a covenant because suddenly the devil had legal rights to the *land* and the Earth, whereas he didn't before. Something got traded in that deal; a covenant of some sort was made.

Sexual sin is the precursor to idolatry.

Folks tend to worship what is good to their flesh. Often, the idol becomes the person that you are having sex, illegally with. Even if the sex is just a fantasy in the mind, sex, flesh, or naked bodies become the idol. Mind sex runs rampant in today's society. Is the sex real or fake? There are 900 numbers for it, the Internet is turning people onto it and opening them up to the *spirit of whoredoms,* which is the *spirit of lust.* This is influencing and infiltrating people's minds. Fantasy after fantasy is playing over in men's heads. Mind sex, fantasy *lust* and virtual sex is also sex. It is also sexual distraction, and it could be what's wrong with your seed and your harvest.

Look at the wisest of men, Solomon. God told him not to marry those strange women because of their strange religions. Next thing you know Solomon has 700 wives and 300 side chicks; I mean concubines. Then Solomon had altars to idle *gods* which we know is abominable to God. Look at this pattern. Covenant, then worship. Sexual sin, then idolatry. Godly Covenant, then worship. Illegal covenant, then idolatry.

God destroyed Sodom and Gomorrah because of sexual sin.

Millions of Israelites were promised an entire and prosperous land, but they fell into murmuring, complaining, idolatry, disobedience, and into sexual sin. See the progression?

Sexual sin is a soul-tie-forming contract that mocks our covenant-making and covenant-keeping God. It dishonors Him and violates our Covenant with Him unless there's much Mercy and Grace shown to us. God says that He is a jealous God and will have no other *gods* before Him. He will not be mocked. God wants to establish and not abolish Covenant.

In the natural, sexual sin has the most stigmata attached to it. It has the most diseases attached to it, both quick, devastating diseases, or slow, tormenting diseases. It can transfer any and every evil *spirit* from one person to another quickly. Let's face it, it's really not worth it. If someone invites you into illegal sex, it's OK to say, *No thank you. I have seed in the ground, and would much rather tend to it than to sin with you and kill my seed.* Or maybe just think it and know it, you don't even have to say it to anyone. Or, you could say, *You know, I'm a parent and I have a son that I need to go minister to.* These are sin-stopping statements.

You should always have seed in the ground, and be harvesting. So, like the farmer at the beginning of this book will stay home during the growing and harvesting seasons instead of being someplace where you shouldn't be.

If Something Offends You

And if thy right hand offend thee, cut it off. It is better for me to enter into life maimed than having two hands. To go to hell. Into the fire that shall never be quenched, (Mark 9:43).

Don't let gangrenous sin and rebellion set in. Don't keep a dead, rotting or nonprofitable part of your life so long that it kills the rest of you. If a member of your body offends you--, if a member of your sowing team offends you, straighten it out and correct it. Get rid of it. Or get it back in order and under authority. If a member of your arsenal is rebellious and out of order, you don't keep it hanging around pretending that it's working properly. If you allow it, it will let you down when you most need it. It may turn on you at the worst time or turn on you in the heat of battle. If you know that the brakes don't work in your car, don't you have them repaired so they will work when you need them?

If a member of your sowing team offends you, if your mind will not comply with the directive to sow, if your Will won't obey your spirit man instead of your emotions or your mind--, if your emotions will not be cheerful when sowing, as they're supposed to be, you have to get that part of you in shape and pretty quick. If a member of your body offends you, it should be cast off, put out, or corrected immediately.

If your mind refuses to obey in the Offering, cast down the imagination where the stronghold of your mind as it imagines that it is higher and wiser than the Word of God. Put the mind of your flesh in its place. Bypass it by making the decision *spiritually*, by accessing the mind of Christ.

If your hand refuses to write the check, use the other hand, and get the cash out of your wallet. If both hands decide to act up, casts their behavior down and call in your offering by telephone. If your Will chooses to be disobedient to God, fast to break the power of the Will and any ungodly strongholds that may be hindering you from participating in the Offering.

Speaking of bypassing, it is neither profitable nor proper to sow a dollar in the offering, unless that is all you have. When you bypass the $20's, $50's, and hundred-dollar bills in your wallet to put a dollar in the Offering, you are not sowing, you are insulting God. You're not insulting the pastor, you're insulting God, and denying the power of the Offering. You're choosing to be a financially broke single rather than a prosperous, multiplying parent.

Of course, it you are trying to insult the pastor, then there is ought there and your Offering seed wouldn't be received by God anyway, so what are we talking about here?

It is also not profitable to make sure you have a beautiful home and all the things you want, but God's house goes lacking because you're not sowing good Offering seeds and ministering to the House of God, (Haggai 1:3 -7).

Selfishness is of the flesh, and the flesh does not profit at all.

For more on low-budget offerings, ***Let Me Have A Dollars Worth*** by this author.

Name Your Seed

When sowing in the Offering, we must name our seed. Naming the seed is a substance of Faith. When a couple is having a baby, when they feel certain that they will, indeed have a baby, they start picking out names. That is a substance of their Faith. Your Offering seed usually already has a name if the anointing for what that Offering should produce was announced by the pastor. If it was not announced, then your prayer should be to ask God, ask Wisdom, what do I name this seed? How much do I sow? What is the harvest for?

We name our seeds so when we talk to God about that Offering, that seed, that *son*, God will need to know *what seed* you're talking about, since you most likely will have more than one seed in the ground.

Note these two things:

1. If you can't name the seed, at least name the Field in which you sowed. Farmers have the Back 40, the South 50, and so on. They name fields by size, location, <u>*and*</u>/or what's planted in them.

Based on the anointing announced at offering time, the pastor may have named the Field everyone was sowing in that day, or you may have a release from God to sow in a particular Field. Is everyone sowing in the Field of Obedience that is announced by the pastor? Or the Field of Pastor-Said-So? What will *that* produce? With faith, just what Pastor said it would.

You sow the seed that corresponds to the Field that you have *authorization* and *anointing* to sow in. Your seed and Field maybe named, **New Car**. It could be named **College Tuition**. It is named whatever you sowed for, and that may be uniquely between you and God.

Do not name your seeds by the amount of money you sowed…that $50 seed or that $120 seed. Call it what you want it to *become*, not what it already **is**. Else, (natural, farm) seeds would be called, Oval Pink Things, Round Brown Things, or Spherical Green Things, descriptive of the seeds rather than the expected harvest. Rather, we call those seeds corn, kale, and sweet peas. Even though they are still *seeds*, we call things what they will be when fully matured.

If we did that with our children, they'd be called baby, child, or toddler all of their life instead of what we expect them to grow into.

2. We don't discuss seed with God by quantity or amount or the day or date we sowed it; that's not His language. He is a God of Faith. We name the seed by its **end result**, by its harvest.

Don't they call your child at school by his last name? What your child is supposed to be when he grows up is not a Christopher or Jasmine, but ultimately your child is supposed to be _____, Jones or Smith --*insert your last name there.* Your child will be called by your last name. So you can say **Seed** is the first name, but the last name is what the harvest is supposed to be when it grows up—corn, collards, et cetera. Call your Offering seed by its last name; that's what faith calls it. Faith calls that seed what it's supposed to be, not what it looks like today.

Faith has *substance.* <u>**Naming your seed** is ***substance***</u>.

Calling your Offering seed, once sown, by it's name that it will be at maturity is also calling it forth. Every time you say My New House, or My New Car, Missions Trip Donation, or Building Fund Money, you are calling that seed forth. You are prophesying to it. You are telling it to be received into that good soil. You are telling it to be watered and nurtured by the Word, by Praise & Worship. You are speaking to the Offering seed, coaxing it, urging it, bringing it forth to be a seedling, reaching for the Sun. You are calling it, son. You are letting it know that you desire that it grow, come into being, come into your life, reach harvest and come into your hands. You are accepting it out of the Spirit, into the natural world. You are welcoming it. You are encouraging it and celebrating it. You are calling it to Purpose, to Ministry, to Destiny.

Prophesy to that seed. Prophesy. Say what GOD says over that Offering and watch your seed grow in stature and favor daily. Amen.

Naming the seeds is a must because when you talk to the Seed, you can't call it $20. dollars; that's not a good name for a *son*. Call it by its name so it can by Faith reach maturity—listen and KNOW the sound of your voice and know that it belongs to **you**!

Bringing in a nameless harvest is difficult to impossible. When a nameless harvest is in, it's a free for all. Anyone could go and get what you sowed for. That might explain where some of your harvests are, lost, ransacked, pillaged, stolen, claimed like a found wallet. Claimed by someone who could vaguely identify it. Someone who could offer a semblance of a name to it may have gotten it. Selah.

Can you imagine the Angels of God having a tug of war with an evil principality in the heavenlies and the Angel of the LORD is saying, give me that $20, it belongs to JimBob. Well, JimBob, you might just get your $20 back. BUT, if the Angel is saying, ***That's JimBob's New House and the Father wants him to have it, wicked principality, stand down….*** See how that's different? Give your Angels something to fight with. Name Your Seed which is the same as saying, Name Your Harvest, because that is Faith.

Begin with the end in mind.

A spiritual lost and found for finances? If there is some random unnamed seeds out there (I suspect a lot), it may explain where you and I have gotten some of our miracle money???

For what are you sowing? Or are you just kidding? Is there a Word over your seed, a Biblical Scripture; was this seed money *anointed* and *sent*? Or are you just wishing and hoping. Even if it wasn't a regular offering, did you get a Word from the LORD before sowing, or were you studying Scripture and the words came alive for you? Yes. **Name your seed**. For what are you believing and what is its name?

Parents in the Bible named their children before they were born, many times before they were ever conceived. Often children's names were given as God announced to parents by angelic messengers that they would soon be with child. I'd like to add that those God-given names were God-given because a child is not something that you own or that you, alone have created. If God speaks to you, prophesies to you, or gives you a promise, it would be wise to go immediately and sow a seed toward that promise. The seed is substance. It is to remind you of the Promise.

Name that seed, the same name as the Promise. It is your earnest. Remember--I won't let go until you bless me.

Anyway, folks did not always wait for the child to be born to name it. Of course, when the gender is not known, that is of concern. Parents who named their children before they are born also prepare a place and a nursery for them. They get the necessary information, instructions, tangible and intangible things to minister to their child. Nameless children such as John and Jane Doe and their cousins. Shaquon and Chiquita Doe do not always reach maturity, either physically, spiritually, intellectually, or emotionally.

Give every seed a blessed name that has a blessed meaning.

Your financial harvest does not have a gender. It's a *son*. So, you can go ahead and name it.

Many times, unnamed children are left orphaned, either physically or emotionally, by their named or nameless parents. An unnamed child is usually not cared about, just as an unnamed seed is usually forgotten.

Name your seed, what's his name? What are you doing to prepare for its arrival at its fullness? Nothing? Wishing or hoping? At least a start planning and expecting. Have you prepared or place for it? Have you made room to receive it? What's its purpose? What's the purpose of it manifesting in the earth? You've sown a seed? Have you named it? Did you name it? Will it be a nameless, orphaned harvest or can anyone go and get it or adopt it? Or is it coming home with you—to you?

A poor harvest is deficient

in whatever way you're deficient.

If you create a sowing journal, you will have to **name your seeds.**

Naming your seed not only says that you have full expectation that it will reach the fullness of harvest, but its name is like putting a *stake* out to help guide it. The stake signals the Seed, instructing it of its name, purpose, calling, destiny. It *becomes* the name. Calling it by its name nurtures the seed into a seedling. The Name instructs the plant to *become* what it's called--, *peas, corn, lima beans*. The Name is the Word for its life. It tells the seed what to become, what to grow up to be. If you have never named a seed, no wonder your seeds have been confused or have had identity issues. They have not known what they're supposed to be--, no different than any child. As you agree with God and prophesy, saying what God says doing what you see your Daddy doing, do you bless yourself by blessing your harvest.

That's what God does. He named you and He certainly and continually calls you by your name and your calling; and He continually blesses you. Having a name circumvents identity crises. Even if the name is just a picture.

When a thing doesn't know what it is, it doesn't know what to do, it can't perform. The Name is the same as putting out a streaked, speckled, or spotted stick right in front of your seed as Jacob did, so it will know how to reproduce itself. Farmers and gardeners do it all the time. They name their seeds; they talk about them. Gardeners talk about how seeds and plants are growing, and many times they have a picture on a little plastic stick in front of the plant to remind them what their seed is supposed to grow into. Really the picture or name on the stake is to remind the gardener of what's planted there that hasn't come up yet, but how do we know it's not God's way of informing the seed of how to grow and what to grow into, as Jacob did with his multiple sticks at the water hole?

Good parents say good things about their growing children all the time.

"*If you can name it, you can govern it. If you can govern it, you can grow it,*" says Prophet Kevin Leal.

Name your seed.

In the 1960s it became popular to talk to your plants. Scientists said that it caused them to thrive and be healthier. Healthier plants produce greater harvest. Once you've named your seed you can call it by its name. *Lord, I thank you for this harvest that's going to pay off my mortgage completely, in Jesus' Name.* I am sure God won't mind if you name your seed, **Pay-Off-My-Mortgage-Completely**. It seems like a very Godly name to me since

Romans 13:8 says, *Owe no man, anything, except to love him.*

Name your seed so you can call it by name as you are encouraging it to thrive and grow. Give it a name so whenever you talk to God about it, He will know what you're talking about.

If the devil tries to steal it—and he will, and you need to lay a claim on your seed, growing or mature, make sure your seed or at least your Field of Blessing, will already have a name.

God does not make mutt-harvests. Whatever your seed is as long as it's nurtured, that is what it'll produce. If it is not nurtured, it will not produce correctly. It could fail completely, producing nothing, or weeds. Whatever the stake is, that's how straight and upright it will be, and whatever its name is, that's what it'll be as long as it's ministered to. However it's nurtured and takes or receives nurturing and correction, like you from God, is how it will produce. Nothing else, outside of a miracle.

Wisdom tells you what to name your seed. Adam used Wisdom to name everything in the garden at Eden.

Motive

Blessed are the pure in heart, for they shall see God in Matthew 5:8

God reads all of our Motives as well as our Faith in what we do, even in sowing seed, in the Offering. We always say that *without Faith it is impossible to please God*, (Hebrews 11:16a). We should also say with a bad Motive it is impossible to please God.

One thing Motive often affects is Faith. If Motive is fleeting or impure, pure Faith cannot back it up. A short burst of faith is good if you wish to blue sky for a while, daydream. Be real, Mustard Seed Faith is necessary for almost any and every spiritual transaction you may need to conduct

Beverly wanted to get a job to earn enough money to buy a stereo system. I had never heard of such. I thought a person would get a job because they wanted a job for a longer term than buying a stereo. I thought a job was a place to do good work, enjoy working there and benefit the boss and the company, as well as yourself. I'd never heard of getting a job and working to buy one particular thing--, especially a stereo system. But this was just the first part of The Beverly Plan. The second part was to quit the job.

If you're just going to sow in the Offering, then quit working or quit the process that comes after the sowing, that also cannot be profitable.

Beverly never got the job, but I did, and thus began my college career of waiting tables in restaurants. In so doing, I earned a lot, learned a lot, and I've written about in **AMONG SOME THIEVES** and other books. My motive was to work the job, help a company, and also earn money. Many times, I would have checks backed up, for weeks, in the office because, being in school, I wasn't available to pick up my checks when the office was open. Getting the money wasn't my sole reason for working, although I was a student, and I could always use the money. But working that particular job has earned me much more than the money that I made. It's even paying me now. I'm still earning on what I learned then, and on what I've sown because my motives were right.

I endured long hours of back-to-back shifts and even insulting customers. One Caucasian man asked me that since I was Black, would I tap dance for him? I nicely put him (his demons) in their place. I could have fainted, become offended, insulted the man and his rowdy friends, and quit the job. But I didn't. I persevered. My motive was to work there and to do it with integrity. This man left me a $50 tip on a $30 check.

The Sower may faint if the desire is not strong, if the motive is not pure and right, if the desire is only fleeting, because no faith will come in to back it up. The Motive must be pure and committed. If it's a motive that is only pure or only determined it cannot reach fruition. It must be both.

And let us not be weary in well doing, for in due season we shall reap, if we faint not,
(Galatians 6:9).

If we faint not, we will reap in due season. If we do not fall into sin, but endure during the growing, maturation, and perfecting process, we will reap. Proper Godly Motive will keep you from *fainting*.

Why do we have to worry about fainting or sinning just because we sowed a seed? Is there a greater temptation because the seed has been sown? Are the enemy's tactics strategically sent against those who have seed in the ground? Yep. The Midianites attacked every spring at the same time, trampling the Israelites' plantings, ruining their harvests, and destroying their increase, (Judges 6:4,6). Why would there be an attack if there's nothing to attack or no hope of spoils to the enemy? When you truly realize who you are, in Christ and what you have, in Him you will understand the enemy's response to you. You will understand, prepare and be ready for any enemy attacks.

The enemy is attacking who you are in the Spirit, not who you are in the natural. Well, that too, but the reason the attacks seem brutal, relentless is because of who you are in the Spirit, who you are to God and in God (Christ). Haven't you ever asked yourself, What is up with this? Why is the enemy still bothering me? I'm not bothering anybody. Oh really? Your words, your presence, your dominion, your authority, whether you know about it or not, whether you use it or not, you are a threat to the devil. Can you hear that Herod, Pharoah's and the like sent out decrees to have all the children under two years old, or all of the firstborn killed? Only unrepentant evil would do such a thing.

As you are saved, but even if you are still a "baby Christian", the devil has issued steal, kill, and destroy orders against you. Neither does the devil want to wait for you to grow up for a fair fight. Mainly because it won't be "fair" anyway, **once you know who**

you really are and get your weapons together you can take him out. He knows this, whether you do or not.

David was still a boy (some say), having to fight an actual giant, Goliath. David wasn't a *boy* in the Spirit. Neither are you – actually. In Christ you are entirely something else. Natural mirrors LIE, they only tell you what you look like to other natural folks; look at yourself in the Spirit, in Christ to see who you really are.

And could it be because you have sowed the seed that the enemy came in?

Yes.

Jesus comes, and usually, it's because you're calling on Him as you're sowing. While Jesus is there, He tends to your seed and to you. He comes to minister to you. He is also there to protect you and your seed from the enemy. Jesus ministers to you because He loves and cares for you and is preparing you to receive your upcoming harvest. As Lord of the Harvest, He is invested in your harvest, so He ministers also to the seed.

He gives seed to the Sower and bread to him who eats (harvest), and multiplies your seed sown, as in the offering, to 30, 60, and 100-fold returns.

Arise & Thresh

Micah 4:13 gives an account of all manner of things coming against the people, even nations, all because of the seed that was sown. How do we know that a seed was sown? Someone is giving birth, travailing, so a seed must have been sown. The enemy will come against you anyway, but especially if you have sown a seed.

If you've made an alliance with the enemy, you cannot very well thresh him, even if the word says so. Your seed is one of the best reasons not to make friends with the enemy.

Not sowing a seed will not keep the enemy from attacking you either. And not sowing a seed cannot protect you from the enemy because the King of Glory will not have a point of contact/covenant to come in. Your seeds are like renewing your covenant with God on a daily or weekly basis, saying, *I won't let go until you bless me.* And He won't let go of that seed until you're blessed.

God likes seeds. God likes *your* seeds. They are your **children**. Jesus said, Suffer the children to come unto Me. Those ***children*** that need to come unto Him can be your financial *sons* that are striving to grow in the Fields of the Lord. The enemy will attack you anyway, but the seeds you've sown in your connection with God--, refreshed. Refreshed seeds connects you with the divine nature of God, **Multiplication** and *Increase* to give you all the things that pertain to life and godliness.

Further when Increase comes it confirms and reconfirms your covenant relationship with God, making you stronger in Him. Just one such transaction with God is powerful enough to empower and strengthen the slightest saint's frail Faith-- establishing Covenant with the Almighty God.

Do you think the enemy really wants you to ever know how you are really hooked up to God?

How many movies have you seen? Here's the usual plot: The leading actor has something to do. It's hard enough. It takes focus and determination, often strength, know-how, and sometimes moxie. If they can only do this thing, it will save the day, satisfy the plot, and make them grow because of having gone through it.

Enter arch enemy. Ideally, you could say that if the person had soul prosperity, they wouldn't have an arch enemy in the natural. Maybe, but the character of the devil will not allow us to make friends with him. Satan cannot be trusted. He is not a covenant maker, he's a covenant breaker, as are any of his unholy.

As in the movie, just as you begin the process of doing the purpose of your life (plot), even if it's by increments, enter the dragon. When all this happens, if your motive for doing it is only fleeting, you may not even fight. Or you may give up or give up just short of winning.

Remember the green grapes of Aesop's fables? Without pure motive and faith to back it up, you may find yourself saying I really didn't want that anyway as you're quitting.

How avidly and ardently you fight the enemy off using the weapons of your warfare will determine how you are able to save your harvest. If you faint, you won't save it at all. If you do some of the spiritual work, maybe you'll receive 30% and so on. When you get really spiritually wise, you will realize that your harvest will manifest abundantly on how well you are able to get the King of Glory, the King of kings, the Lord of lords, the Lord of the Harvest, to come in and protect your seed and your *return,* some 30, some 60 and some 100-fold.

Just the Two of Us

Let me say it again. You've sown correctly, spirit-to-Spirit. You've created something or connected to something that was awaiting the sowing of your seed. The seed seemed to be yours because God gave it to you and entrusted it with you with it to sow. Now that you've sown it and He's *received* it, it seems that it should belong to Him again, and that He will send it back to you, *Increased* in a special way.

But right now, that seed belongs to both of you. No one has a child alone. It takes two. That seed now belongs to both of you. Jesus has a vested interest in your seed, maybe more than you do, since He avers that He does not want one to be lost. Here, we believe that means souls, but it also means anything He puts His hand to. As God knows the numbers of hairs on your head, the number of stars, sands, and jots and tittles (Matthew 5:18) that don't fall to the ground unless he knows it, surely, He knows all about your seed, especially seed that He has *received*. He won't let go until you let go.

Taking that deeper, you are the planting of the Lord, (Isaiah 61:3). When you plant a fruit tree, it produces fruit. The fruit also has seeds. You're supposed to have seeds, often, and regularly, seasonally. If you have fruit, you will have seeds. If you don't have fruit, you will not have seeds. If you don't have seeds, you won't have fruit. The fig tree did not have fruit and was cursed, (Mark 11:13-21). If you are not sowing regularly, if you're not reaping abundantly, you may be under the same curse that we spoke of earlier. *Unfruitfulness* and *untruthfulness* lead to death. But as you have sowed seeds as God, Jesus, and the Holy Spirit is ministering to you, *you are also ministering to your seed.* You're doing what you see God do. You minister to your natural seeds, your financial seeds, as well as your spiritual seeds.

Naturally, you minister to souls, and you went through evangelism as well. You tend to your personal finances.

That you have seed in the ground speaks of contract, covenant, agreement, and purpose with God. It means not only that He's providing for you, but also that you're going somewhere in *Him*. And seed is His way of providing for your future as well. Do you think the enemy likes that? Of course not. You better get your spiritual weapons and fight.

After your sowing has been *received*, you and Jesus are now ministering to the same seed, you, in the natural, Jesus in the Spirit.

Determination to reach a desired end, to finish your victory and success is a good Motive, but of all the Motives, the best one, by far, is Love. Love is better than anything. It will keep you afloat, alive, and faint free.

Though I speak with the tongues of men and angels and have not charity I am become a sounding brass or a tinkling cymbal. 1 Corinthians 13:1

And though I bestow all my goods to feed the poor, and though I give my body to be burned, and have not charity, it profiteth nothing. 1 Corinthians 13:3

    It is easy to know if you're moving in Love or not. If your purpose in sowing or any dealings that you have with anyone is only with the thought of *what's in it for me*, then that's not Love. If you are willing to scorch the Earth to get what you want, to get your way, even if you call it blessings, doesn't make it pure Motive. If you aren't looking at a win-win situation, for all parties involved, then, it's not Love. And it's not a pure Motive.

    If you reach the point of desperation, it's hard to sow in Love, because desperation overrides the pure Motive, emotion, and action of Love. Desperation also pulls you into idolatry, desperate measures, desperate actions, the model of the idolater. This could be why many 'saints' don't receive from their sown seeds. They've waited too late to sow them. They may have been out in battle and have returned home to frantically find no harvest when they desperately need a harvest. So, they sow a seed for a tree, but wanted to grow overnight. Only the devil makes these kinds of promises in lotteries and casinos.

Desperation is not a season for sowing. God is Provident. Provident does not just mean that He provides, it means He provides well before the harvest is needed. The Lamb was slain *before* the foundation of the world. Our Father is not last minute. He's not an 11th hour God. He's merciful and provides miracle money, which I call *mercy money*, but that is not how the Just are supposed to be living.

I'm saying this again because it's important. Having Mustard Seed Faith means that you don't take no for an answer if God says the answer is, Yes. Mustard Seed Faith is not a teeny tiny amount of faith. It is not the short burst of faith that we see in desperation, and needy, wanting people. Mustard Seed Faith is enduring, persevering, I'm-going-to-reach-my-destination kind of faith. Pure motives draw this kind of faith. God is looking at your Motive, the enemy is looking at your Motive also, and he's planning an attack based on how weak or corrupt it is.

When Motive is pure and determined, then Mustard Seed Faith will come and you will outlast, and even defeat the enemy.

Aside: most of the mustard plants growing the USA is grown in Idaho, North Dakota, Montana, Oregon, and Washington in harsh conditions. Mustard Seeds might be small, but they are very hardy. Canada is the world's leading producer of mustard seed, and we know winters can be long and cold that far north.

Can you muster the courage to endure? With the right motive, Faith will come, and you will endure. And if you do persevere, you will prosper. Your seed will blossom abundantly.

Balancing It All

You need to have the right spirit in you to hook up to the divine in order to experience any fold and especially 30, 60, or 100-fold. Your spirit-to-God's Spirit covenant creates *life*. A living seed prospers. The longer it lives, the more it bears, and with proper cultivation, fertilization, and pruning, the more productive it's harvests are.

Humility should be balanced with assurance. Assurance is good. It's necessary. Blessed assurance--, being fully persuaded. Confidence is the next step up from that.

Undisciplined confidence leads to a spoiled child. *I know my dad is going to do it for me*. Do this for me and that for me. *My daddy does whatever I say*. That's confidence, alright, so confidence must be tempered with humility and right desire.

Jesus could have been a spoiled brat. Why wasn't He? Humility. (And buffeting of which Paul speaks, 2 Corinthians 12:7.) Humility is a right assessment of yourself. (A man ought not to think more highly of himself than he ought, (Romans 12:3)). Again, calling for balance.

The world calls humility a meekness of spirit, so if you have the world's definition of humility and humility only, you'd be too spiritually timid. In that case, you won't sow, but you would give. Giving implies handing something over to someone, and old something, possibly to any old one, as discussed before. Sowing is directed placement of something appropriate, appropriately placed. It also implies that the appropriately placed something is *received*. Direct placement requires relationship and if reproduction is involved, relationship requires intimacy. Relationship may start out with giving, but in the natural the hand ain't multiplying nothing. Balance your simple giving with giving toward the intent of intimacy. Folks do it all the time when they are dating--, flowers, cards, candy, simple gifts hopefully, all leading to intimacy.

If you spread some birdseed, birds will come. Seeds draw. They draw increase in prosperity to you over time, but they also draw predators. Spiritual seeds draw spiritual predators. The Book of the Revelation talks about a dragon prepared to devour a child as soon as it was born. (Revelations 12:4). Your spiritual and financial seeds are yummy to the devil; so it takes courage to sow.

Sowing your money is as a gift to God. Because you have a relationship, and because you desire intimacy, you desire Him to receive your gift. Money as a seed draws whether it's sown or not, but at least when it's sown into God's hands we've got protection for it, I summarize. It takes courage to sow.

It takes Ignorance and arrogance not to sow.

Receiving proper *returns* in the Offering is by more than obedience. It's by more than experience, financial backing, or having a lot of money to sow, as in overloading a slot machine, thinking it will eventually pay out, and you'll be there. That theory doesn't work either. It's by more than the mechanics of giving, giving, giving. It's by more than the work of giving. It is by faith and by right faith, with purpose and right motive.

Works without faith is *only work*. You work on your job as the world rewards you for just work. But even at work you have faith you are going to get paid, else you wouldn't go.

Faith without works is dead. Dead faith does not bring 30, 60, or 100-fold return in your sowing. Balancing all of this has been and will be presented in this book as a noble task for your soul and *spirit man*. With the Holy Spirit, Wisdom can be accessed. Since the Lord hates a false balance, it's an abomination to Him, if you're attempting to reach balance, with God's help this will prove very profitable.

Delivery Charges Apply

This chapter will be connected to ***Power Money: Nine Times the Tithe*** in a much closer way than any preceding chapters. Read that book if you haven't.

Who will Deliver? It seems you've been expecting forever; who will Deliver? Seeds have been sown; they've been received, now it's time for harvest. You've been expecting this harvest for so long. *Who will deliver?*

Worship God so He will come into your presence, or you can come into His, because you are going to need Him to Deliver this seed that has matured. He is Lord of the Harvest!

You need a Deliverer for your seed because the Devourer is perched, waiting to consume and destroy, even devour it.

The dragon stood in front of the woman who was about to give birth, so that it might devour her child the moment he was born.
Revelations 12:4b

Seedtime & Harvest is a spiritual law, it cannot be violated. Who will deliver your seed? Your harvest? You? Are you going to do it? By yourself?

I cannot teach all of what's in **Power Money: Nine Times the Tithe** in a few pages, but as Seedtime & Harvest is a Law that cannot be violated, I must clear up sowing in the Offering for those who don't tithe. I have said in books previous, that you can't participate in the Offering if you don't tithe. But Seedtime & Harvest remains. So, for your consideration: As you sow a seed, based on any and all of the criteria discussed and outlined in this book are met, your seed may be *received* and may actually reach fruition and fullness. But who will Deliver? How will those blessings, that harvest get to you? *Who will Deliver?* One can sow in the Offering, but without first tithing one cannot _**receive**_ from the Offering.

The Lord is showing me a vision. I see a huge supply of whatever you need, money, cash , houses, cars – whatever you've sowed for stacked up-- , for days!!! All that harvest is stuck, as it were, in a warehouse or a holding center. There is no one to Deliver it if you are not a tither. In the non-tither's life, there are *Delivery charges* that have not been paid. The person who Delivers these items has to go through treacherous territory. They have to climb mountains (your doubt) wade through rivers (your uncertainty) ski snowy slopes (slippery faith) and jump across dangerous ravines (gaps in your fragmented soul and sketchy worship). It takes a powerful, skilled, and anointed person to make this **Delivery**; it takes an anointing to make your Delivery. Why? Because what is being Delivered is very valuable, you are very valuable and… there is a spiritual and financial war going on against the saints of God.

Who are we kidding? The enemy doesn't want you to receive anything from God. Nothing. Not the answer to a prayer, not sun to shine on you, not water to drink, food to eat or any other blessing. He wants you out of communication with God. The Devil will send demonic angels to withstand Angels of Blessings that are trying to DELIVER answers to prayer, blessings, miracles, comfort, peace, you name it! This describes the war, it's for any and all things that God has planned for your life or things that God gives for your life and godliness. So you know finances are a biggie, a big deal and of great interest to all.

Who is the enemy waging the war? The Devourer.

Who is the only one who can Deliver the goods to you? ***The Tithe***. The Tithe is as a Delivery Anointing put in all *Increase*. There is a tithe in EVERY Increase. When you are not working the Tithe, it won't be working for you. The Tithe gets you into the Fold, identifying you as a person who, if they *parent* their seed to 30, 60, and 100-Fold can receive

Delivery on it. And it brings the *Increase* to you. (Read **Power Money: Nine Times the Tithe** to better understand this chapter.)

As long as Seedtime & Harvest remains, you can sow and grow 30, 60, and 100-fold increase, but you won't receive it if there is no Delivery Service. Just as with your newspaper, or your telephone service, there will be service interruption due to non-payment.

Conversely, there are big, heavyweight, heavy duty trucks lined up, revved up, ready to go, but there is nothing on them. These trucks are the vehicles that will bring Increase to the saints that tithe, but don't sow in the Offerings. We learned in *Power Money: Nine Times the Tithe* that the Tithe will always get to you with its accompanying reward. But the higher increases of 30X, 60X and 100X need a bigger Delivery vehicle to make the Delivery. Too many "saints" do not sow in the Offering, they only tithe. Some have Delivery trucks awaiting to deliver things to them, but they have no cargo to deliver because no Offering was sown.

"Saints" who have sowed in the Offering have much cargo, but no *means* of receiving it because they haven't tithed —they haven't paid the Delivery charges. God's plan is that those who tithe, have a way to receive from Him and those who give Offerings have something to receive and that His system is to be worked to the full, not ala carte, not partially.

Did you know this? Wisdom does.

Recommended book: **Power Money: Nine Times the Tithe**

https://a.co/d/9uwB9VP

Recommended mini book **When The Devourer Is Rebuked** both by this author https://a.co/d/aJbjZ2J

Dear Reader:

Thank you so much for acquiring and reading this volume. I pray it has blessed you and that you can use information contained in it. See you in the next book!

Love,
Dr. Marlene Miles

Dr. Marlene Miles has served in Ministry for 20+ years. She holds two doctorate degrees in Ministry and is a dentist by day. Her joy is to share what God gives her.

Enjoy her messages on the Dr. Miles YouTube Channel.

Christian books by this author:

AK: Adventures of the Agape Kid

AMONG SOME THIEVES

As My Soul Prospers

Behave

Churchzilla (Wanna-Be Bride of Christ)

The Coco-So-So Correct Show

Demonic Cobwebs

Demonic Time Bombs

Demons Hate Questions

Do Not Orphan Your Seed

Do Not Work for Money

Don't Refuse Me Lord

Every Evil Bird

The FAT Demons

got Money?

Let Me Have a Dollar's Worth

Living for the NOW of God

Lord, Help My Debt

Lose My Location

Made Perfect In Love

The Man Safari *(I'm Just Looking)*

Marriage Ed., *Rules of Engagement & Marriage*

Motherboard: *Key to Soul Prosperity*

My Life As A Slave

Name Your Seed

Plantation Souls

The Poor Attitudes of Money

Power Money: Nine Times the Tithe

The Power of Wealth

Seasons of Grief

Seasons of War

SOULS in Captivity

Soul Prosperity: Your Health & Your Wealth

The *spirit* of Poverty

This Is *NOT* That

The Throne of Grace, *Courtroom Prayers*

Warfare Prayer Against Poverty

When the Devourer is Rebuked

The Wilderness Romance

Other Journals & Devotionals by this author:

The Cool of the Day – Journal

got HEALING? Verses for Life

got HOPE? Verses for Life

got WISDOM? Verses for Life

got GRACE? Verses for Life

got JOY? Verses for Life

got LOVE? Verses for Life

He Hears Us, Prayer Journal

I Have A Star, Dream Journal

I Have A Star, Guided Prayer Journal,

J'ai une Etoile, Journal des Reves

Let Her Dream, Dream Journal *in colors*

Men Shall Dream, Dream Journal,

My Favorite Prayers (in 4 styles)

My Sowing Journal

Tengo una Estrella, Diario de Sueños

Illustrated children's books by Dr. Miles

Big Dog (8-book series)

Do Not Say That to Me

Every Apple

Fluff the Clouds

I Love You All Over the World

Imma Dance

The Jump Rope

Kiss the Sun

The Masked Man

Not During a Pandemic

Push the Wind

Tangled Taffy

What If?

Wiggle, Wiggle; Giggle, Giggle

Worry About Yourself

You Did Not Say Goodbye to Me

www.ingramcontent.com/pod-product-compliance
Lightning Source LLC
Chambersburg PA
CBHW071315060426
42444CB00036B/2878